A Well-Tuned Harp

Geraldine C. Little

Saturday Press, Inc. 1988

Acknowledgement is made with thanks to the publications in which the following poems first appeared, sometimes in slightly different form: "Manse," "Watching Sailboats," *Nimrod;* "Early Spring in the Pine Barrens," "Lasting Resonance," *Stone Country;* "Mama Out of Donegal," *Saturday's Women;* "Dining Room," *Poetry Miscellany;* "Scullery," *Greenfield Review;* "A Brother Dies of Lupus," "Creek Rites," *Seneca Review;* "Illuminated Page: Kellsian Fragment," *The Literary Review;* "Birches: Peterborough, New Hampshire," *Images;* "Pulpit," *Green Mountains Review;* "One Kind of Bestiary," "For Venice, Sinking," *Poetry Northwest;* "Canzone for Constellations," *Prize Poems,* National Federation of State Poetry Societies, Inc.; "Message to Other Civilizations: Bach," *Milkweed Chronicle;* "Version: Old Tale after the Grimms," *Blue Unicorn;* "The Exceptional Child," *Journal of New Jersey Poets;* "Picture of Victims of Famine," *Poets for Africa;* also appeared in *Lip Service;* "Looking at a Pompeian Lady in an Exhibit," "A Viewer, Scotland," *Poet Lore;* "Dover, the Present Time, Looking Towards Dunkirk," *St. Andrews Review;* also won the Gordon Barber Award, Poetry Society of America; "Ballade by an Old Jewish Woman," *Jewish Currents;* "Poem for Charlotte Mew," *Bitterroot;* "Schooldays at the University of Alabama," *South Street Star;* "Illuminations: Fish" is reprinted with permission from *Yankee Publishing;* "From the Top of the RCA Building" is reprinted from *Prairie Schooner,* by permission of University of Nebraska Press, copyright © 1977 University of Nebraska Press.

Saturday Press wishes to thank Martin Ritter, the Columbia Cheese Corporation, the Schering-Plough Corporation, and other contributors whose generous support has made possible the publication of this book.

Library of Congress Cataloging in Publication Data

Little, Geraldine Clinton.
  A well-tuned harp.

  I. Title.
PS3562.I7828W45 1988 811'.54 87-28838
ISBN 0-938158-09-0 (pbk. : alk. paper)

Cover and design by Susan Quasha

SATURDAY PRESS, INC.
P. O. Box 884
Upper Montclair, NJ 07043

For
Louisa Margaret Corr Clinton
and
James Robert Clinton, D.D.

CONTENTS

I

II

III

I

Lasting Resonance

Listen, I can't help it. Sundays of my childhood
Father perched in the pulpit box, releasing
majestic, sonorous birds of language, the King
James version of miracles and mythologies, over my head
like a beautiful plague that struck me down forever.
How shall I learn to put away childish things,
to conjure the world in the innocent speech of the sparrow,
whose bones fleshed under the shadows of eagles?

Pulpit

Of bog oak black as sin preached against,
polished, it rides the church on the cliff toppling
to the North Sea like a curagh tensed
in wind partial to shoals and unstable currents.

A child sits in the last pew. A window
is open to the summer sea's gentler anthems.
On the rocky beach another child's yellow
pail upturned spills castles out like wishes

granted. There is the moat spanned by a clamshell
drawbridge, the stick with scrap-paper standard fluttering,
great walls of sand thrust up against fell-
ing waves. The impulse is always to delay disaster.

The child inside, impatient with words spinning
in whirlpools sucking her ever closer to hell
radiantly drawn, strains to enter the ring
of romance and fancy the beach child magically works

in sand *she's* been told sinks. Oh let it sink
with her barefoot prints to ribaldries of fishermen mending
nets, kites dashing above nest-stuffed chinks
in the chalky expanse straggling to watery patterns

tides tat, and birds' elegant passions.
What she remembers is the lifeline back to the boat
eddying in nothing understood, the urgent fashion-
ing, in her head, of cargos of weeks impenitently secular.

Singing the Dream

In a small shop in Ireland, my grandfather
is tapping nails into a shoe, his honorable trade.
Gulls clatter along the coastline.
In her cluttered parlor my grandmother
is playing hymns on the pump organ.
This is a long time ago
I have walked into out of the din
of America.
        I pull up a chair
beside my grandmother. I begin to sing.
She doesn't hear me, for *she* is singing
to my mother sweet in her womb, she
who will move among daisies and primroses,
a young girl with no thought
that I am waiting for her
to hold me, as she dies,
a long shuddering moment, before she returns
to my grandmother's otherworldly music
I am listening to in the salt-touched air
of a green place, my grandfather setting the meter
for dreaming.

Now Granny moves
from Godsongs to the brown teapot,
pours out the substance
of our lives.

Manse

Like a great grey box set on a carpet of saffron
primroses, it stared solidly at the North Sea
slapping the cliff the church beside it crowned.
What does the baby alone on an island of quilt
(her Grandmother's, worked in another beginning) know
of factions and clacking sects in North Ireland air
innocent, that captured spring, as the camera's eye
blinked by a mother who shortly will sail to America?

It is all curlews crying, a trembling oak dappling
an Aunt winded from a walk up the cliff, come
for tea in the dining room defined by lack
of space: unmatched chairs drawn up to the scarred
table white linen hides, linen lit by candlesticks
curiously ornate, silvery salvers of scones,
cream puffs and lemon tarts, a compote of trifle
secularly sherried, one small parlormaid starched
taut as the tablecloth, rear bow bobbing under
framed proverbs and portraits in turf-fire-smoked oils.

And always the good bread, homemade and brown,
blessed by the child's father, celluloid collar
not choking realms of memorized Biblical heights
he relates easily as a camel crosses a desert.
Spoons resonate on genteel china, talk
is uneasily light in gaps when the minister sips
tea wickedly black and addresses three-minute eggs.

This is the later-told-tale the baby is sure
she really remembers. Listen, she can tell you how tiny
bright shadows fell on the primroses' greenery,
can call up conversation heard through an open pane,
its upper square shivery with candlelight she cannot reach,
can draw dimensions of the stranded rectangle of blanket
whose borders she cannot cross, can sketch the curlews
screaming, screaming, into too imminent darkness.

From the Top of the RCA Building, New York City

you tipsy out of the Rainbow
Room to the roof eight hundred
gulping feet over
the boroughs. To the left
a helicopter hangs
like a dun dragon-
fly over the Pan-Am
perpendicular steel
stream. Pin people
glint like motes on skeins
webbing to water. A liner
toys past Liberty lustering
moth ball clouds. Here
you see it plain: the small
island taut between currents
whorling to sea. Words
spin from the statue in a tangle
of tongues. You tilt
back into rainbow, reeling
at the depth of perspective, the tricks
on the eye   on the ear   the huddle
calling their nameless names

Mama Out of Donegal

       Hands
are the center of the story.
       Nothing like moths or the Monarch
now flaming to sea on faith.
       Small, worked
           weblike over
           supple muscle

(six children the workers of webs)

       Listen. Her world is black & white
keys, the press of pedals. London
       and a College of Music move
           fingers like firesparks. We read
reviews: England, Scotland, Ireland
       great halls glowing.

       Before I was married, she thunders
Rachmaninoff, Bartok, Scriabin
       the room of her own we sit in
           silent, listening to waterfalls,
               quick-eyed birds & lizards
                  daisies just coming to belief.

       It was a winter of blaze:
sunfall on frost. And the dark illness
       crept in, furnished
           her bright rooms for a long stay,
              the longer dying.

       Sometimes in firelight
I form shadow creatures with my hands.
       Nothing like hers.
           It's the webs I can't weave
that I would like to play
       like a well-tuned harp.

Treasurer of My Father's Church

He was the man, plump as a blown-up balloon,
pompous in tailor-made suits
(stuffs from England, he'd work
like necessary threads
into any conversation, hands
hooked like medals
into popping seams of his waistcoats),
who practised juggling
coins and important paper
in the building downtown
I thought dour as a rainy day without books;
grey, endless, nothing like
the Victorian grandeur of his home
(all bows and candles, wreath-looped lamps,
paisley cloths on numerous tables
cluttered with glittering framed people
unreal to me as miles of rooms fraught
with ponderous furniture)
we were summoned to for dutiful dinners,
servants at crisp-aproned attention,
carving knives flourished
like dueling swords
above roasts and silver-dished vegetables.

Such expertise
could be banked on
in Depression days
to float the church
like an ark
through flooding waters
to solvency's Ararat.

Just once
I heard my father cry.
Hidden behind the half-open door
of his study, I heard his voice

break, like a corner of stained glass
hit at just the right angle to shatter
the whole,
on the words

*why must I beg again for my check
again overdue a week?*

What does a child know,
youngest of six all at home?

Father, I never have found
any dove returned,
any olive branch
that could cover
the slivered wounds
of such nakedness.

Roof

Consider the challenge: topping the grey austere walls
of the church set in a confluence of wildflowers, the yard
laden with saintly (or sinnerly) bones to the right
of panels holding, in stained-glass light, scenes
of Biblical miracle wrought lyrically, the slate
roof slid to a broadish perimeter pigeons prowled
for wanton seeds or windblown anything edible.
It summoned two girls, elevenish, to stare upward
to the avenue of adventure, to the possibility of walking
round, at angel height, turrets of God.
Under cloistered corridors, doors stood open to need.
How cold the belltower stone steps, how worn
and webbed, how clanging their whispers on the climb
to freedom in the form of a square of light farther than faith
in the bravado vows of courage to conquer taken
in the evening-primrosed and sparrowy grasses below.
But they stepped into late sunlight flashing on slate
quivering with shadows of oaks, maples, shivering,
tingling with thrill of temptation not vanquished. They remember
the inching almost endless half crawl on the fragile precipice,
their father's house three fields away minimized,
the odd leveling with leaf and indifferent birds,
the taut nerve frantically (secretly) clutched.
How taken-for-granted, once, was achievement of heights!
In lowering light doves returned to hard pastures,
squirrels thumped on, clung to, slopes. I never see
them descend. They are always hand-in-hand by the belltower
the whole perimeter absorbed, and far below
cornflowers are darkening, lights are ticking on
under the canopies of comfort eternally longed for.

Dining Room

Like an objet d'art an outboard motor
embellished one corner just beyond
the ironing board kept up all day,
not always downed for dinner. Only
a freshet of guests insured its folding —
for only space. One half a cloth
was turned back on itself. Half
bared, the table was the womb
of Father's sermons, scribbled while
Mother creased his Sunday suit,
a damp cloth hissing in sharp lines.
Mother, who took most meals with book
propped up and swallowed the library's manna,
followed "soaps" with each smooth sweep
of iron, rapt at mangled lives.
"Those weeping women," Father scowled
but did not move. Not since have I
heard sermons throbbing out full throttle,
nor dined in any halls awash
with such a cluttered, certain love.

Scullery

It is autumnal light always flares through windows
looking to remnants of an apple orchard: two trees
strung with worm-drilled fruit whisper in a breeze
a woman in an apron outlined in violet rick-rack
remarks on: *winter soon.* In the scullery tacked
like a down-and-out relative to the kitchen, fudge
is the memory-in-the-making, bubbling and aromatic
as a child's belief in everlasting now. From a silver spoon
a sample is dropped in a tumbler of cold water prisming
the rough pine wall, the child's eyes
expectant as a faun's at a teat.
Will it ball or stray in spidery threads of error?
This is the moment she hears, in the stretched silence,
jays, cardinals, sparrows, probing for provender
against bone-known barrenness, hears late bees
in ragged hollyhocks that rap, rap
on the thin pane as if asking for entrance,
all things straining towards salvation's hearth.
The globe holds! Holds the released breath
as the woman bends to shape sweetness to substance
and the rick-rack in dimming light changes
to purple deep as shadows on appletrees the child
will climb, in spring, until invisible in blossoms
presaging *fruit, fall,* in the shed's stark clarity.

Orange

Winter light spears through clouds ambivalent
and dour: to release or hold snow ecstatically
wanted by a child descending to presents
randomly piled, train tracks running
only in circles around the pine tree redolent
of Maine in mid-summer (wildflowers, bear, great rocks
garnished with sea-spray), the tiny village absent
of light till the child plugs into unseen power
and the village winks in the wintery dawn. The tree
is wild with color. No careful scheme of only
blue and silver. Scant money, this rainbow whee
indicates, odd lights and balls never discarded.
A small hand reaches for her father's sock dangling
over the still dark fireplace. She cannot, does not,
wait for parents, siblings. In an armchair strangling
in time, tapestried elegance dying, the child
empties the weave of a stern foot's passage, except
for the sphere in the toe. Juncos bounce in her bones.
It is there, really there. Slowly she draws it out,
the globe of childhood at rest on her palm,
a bauble come from a Wise Man's chest, pale ocher
at the poles, girth beamingly ruddy, calm
green flecks like tiny oases in a sun-stunned desert.
Camels bawl, stomp, nip, bells sing,
sigh to overtones, women's veils whisper,
gossip, doves fidget and drone. Where a spring
pools, beasts lap over their grateful shadows.
Someone is dancing. Dust flares in the cold
room where the child rubs magic against her cheek.
She flies on the odor of fruit, rare and old,
to the top of the tree tipped by a rickety star.
It *is* snowing now. *How easily dreams once came true!*
The drowsy family drifts in. The child in the chair
all day will travel in simple glory avenues
of light. She will not let go the orange. Not ever.

Icehouse

Cold says to winter's molecules: *freeze*
and the stream goes into the magical block we tricycled
almost a mile to see a muscled man ease
from the red brick castle to a platform simmering in summer.

The forbidden: nearly always the best tale
in a child's book. It's clear what my mother feared.
Distance from fenced-in safety, an improbable gale,
that someone would snatch us on the treacherous journey.

I don't know why the hoop of the tongs, sun
glinting off them (curved swords) didn't send us pedalling
back like prodigals, but wasn't that half the fun,
the tingling fright in the gut, the thin ice skated?

Then God in his dirty plaid shirt chopped us a sliver,
wrapped in old newsprint, we sucked in the leafy heat,
the idle bird-songed summer, fingers shivering splendidly in the riotous rushing stream

stilled for us knowing nothing of how chunks melt
until only sharp tongs lie on the windblown sawdust.

Sensory

When others clattered in the kitchen after dinner
I liked to nuzzle close to the golden radiator
taller than I, at right angles to the window
facing an alley between Miss Renard's house and ours.
There was always a pan of bread dough set
on the segmented warmth. Like a cradled baby
covered with linen carried from the house
on an Irish coast, the body grew, grew, pungently
summoning. Moonlight braved the alleyway,
made radiant the silver receptacle, the snowy cloth,
the flaking gold paint.

        I watched Miss Renard
signing to John, her deaf son, a secret incantation.
In the maple tree behind our houses, an owl blessed
unseen offerings. The radiator rattled, bubbled, hissed.
I pressed my innocence to the shining heat, watched
shadowy fingers speak behind Miss Renard's suddenly
snapped-down shade. *Was it scolding or sweetness
went on in the moon-touched silence?*

I wonder tonight as an owl sinks to the top
of the pine tree, signing with fingery wingtips
against the moon, fall earth savory
as risen bread, creature sounds in the night
immense and holy in the hearing,
in the hearing, the hearing.

Creek Rites

Almost defeated by city heat
we drove there, to swim.
From the grassy treeless bank
we'd push off to the other.
The color of the creek was brown; it was
peaceful, opaque water over-
hung on one side by mazes
of trees we couldn't name, and clotted
brush. We swam through shadows of high
fragrant greenery to where a rope dangled
from a flower-spangled tree, two sisters
free of parenting too proper
for our fancies.

Shinnying up, once, I felt something,
rubbed by bark, between my thighs
explode to a field crazy with sun
and flowers whose petals all were stars
I lay on moaning, mooning.
Almost, almost, I fell away
to only prickly brush before
strangling the branch with frantic love.

Hang on the rope. Hurry. Dazed
with what I didn't know
I grasped the thick tickling coil
my sister began to swing, bells
in my head donging dizzy changes,
at last, over the receptive water,
dropped through air heavy with summer
stillness, into my shadow floating
among lilies one dragonfly iridesced.

Still I recall how there was nothing
behind the shape I fractured, nothing
but cold and clutching roots. Then

I popped into my bones, flesh
like a secret found
in moist, mysterious depths.

A Brother Dies of Lupus

He had no heritage of wolves.
Lambs, and fish prancing,
a cat holding blown clouds
in eyes the color of grass.

The double helix is a forest
of feasibilities. Look
how my hands are not Holbein's,

only my own stroking
the tamed peregrine, or bitten
by packs of mad dogs.

There were no howls to hear
thin on crystalline air,
shattering even strong limbs.

The single one first, silhouette
stark against the sky. You
might even offer it meat, a bed.

Satisfaction is nothing
understood. The hill beyond the hill
is the one wanted, it

already dissolving
to the one ahead.
Meat, bedding, never enough.

Reserves were called up, yowled
down the coil: *more, more*
fanged out on frosted breath.

The feast was an orgy
of organs: liver, kidneys,
the tasty heart.

We suppose them to have slunk
back. We think we hear them,
nights, in wilds of spiral,

whimpering they're still hungry,
why don't we feed them.
And someone will,
someone will.

Watching Sailboats

for another brother, a minister

There's something clean about sailboats.
Shipshape, trim, those orderly adjectives

we can rarely apply to life. I watch
white triangles stagger and hold. Why

is *loss* the word identifying class
even at this distance? I see you

anchored and happy, wetting a line
for anything that flashed in scaly flesh.

You never believed in rowboats
for fishing. No. You wanted to sail,

tacking hard to deeps
you believed in, reeling slowly

surely, overcoming luffs, snapped masts
breaking brittle as the heart

we never knew, you never said,
was faulty as a flawed centerboard.

The sudden sinking. Quiet. No storm,
except for ours howling *no no*

to indifferent winds that take
whatever they can get for fuel.

In this circle of pines and sea
I hold your narrow volume of poems.

All about fishing. How you believed
a star could hook men to heaven.

Near Miss

Lolling in a tub, languid
as Marie Antoinette before the fall
I idly soap the familiar
arrondissements of my body.

What is the strange small hill,
quite new in this district,
on the promontory
of my left breast?

Fleet as rain slithering down
a pane
I consult inspectors
green-gowned as doctors.
Out of place, they pronounce.
No permission given for this project.

> Is this structure a cancer
> obstructing all avenues
> of escape?

> Who is weeping
> into the wind
> all the way, all the way
> home?

Then the removal machine
I am sure will gape a hole
ugly, untouchable.

When I return
from a foreign country
an angel is whispering.
She translates:
benign, a blessing
I swallow, feel its fire

burn me to life
I tongue like a new lover.

Inside my nifty negligee
whose label is *joie*
I pin a note for remembrance:

black smoke can smother.
Like that. Just
like that.

Abortion

Swift-running river,
floating orange peels
tossed from a pail,
careless refuse
of the city.

Yesterday
he peeled
the quickening, tossed
it in a pail;
he termed it tissue.

Here from the bridge
I watch the currents.
Orange peels blur,
assume small faces
bobbing bodiless.

The very hairs
on our head are numbered,
someone said
in another country: water
under the bridge.

White strings stream
from the peels, curl
in the swilling wake.
I try to count them,
the numbered hairs

of a careless coition.
They disappear and I
am left with the dead
bones of moon,
its veneer of shine.

Maple

So this is what pain is, the harsh drone
of a saw tearing off limbs you tell me
are cancerous even to death. What can we believe?

Here are leaves like kaleidoscope chips
flung from the wounded mother, settling
on the porch unmasked by lack
of fifty-year shadows. I gather an armful
of hues on fire. Nothing to do with fall
just pressing towards winter.
I think if I shake them
three boys in ripped jeans will shinny up
to the chuckle of robins ordering the world again
to beginnings. A squirrel will scatter bees
they may or may not avoid as they climb
towards the top and believe they are conquering
everything, forever. To the left a hawk
slides slow circles far above bulbs
showing bits of breast to the rain
not yet hurrying the climbers' descent.

Shake and they're tall, tall,
spinning up trees academic and corporate,
scattered like leaves I clutch
as if I could hold
in the kaleidoscope's circle
always
children in the perfect tree
nothing could grind
to dust.

Slippage

*"The mysteries of the faith cannot be either
affirmed or denied; they must be placed above that
which we affirm or deny."*

SIMONE WEIL

Father, Mother, you embraced
Weil, her transcendent goodness. I try
to sit on the sky, to see

what you saw, secure in the Cross
and bloodied Lamb, but I fall
again and again into the wilderness

of brain cells and synapses
that tell me God
may be a woman used to crosses,

the monthly blood shed,
the white wings
of clothes repetitively strung,

may be the silken wing
of a bee at a rose, the rose itself
anointed with rain,

the globe of an apple
hanging against the moon,
the moon advancing, retreating,

may be light from a star born
before Christ clutched it,
is never the Father

hands full of cancer and poverty
of flesh and spirit pacing
the world's four winds.

I whisper denial, deny
the high throne of His sky
but affirm my place

on earth, its muddy stench,
its rutting masses, those mysteries
sufficient for a lifetime's labor.

Yet I wonder, Simone, Mother,
Father, how did you manage
the cosmic leap

I long for when I am sucked,
sometimes, into the black hole
beyond cells and senses?

Early Spring in the Pine Barrens, New Jersey

Tentative syllables of green. I think
    how the whole story will unfold, think
how the pitcher plant I canoe towards
    in its room beneath canes of wild blueberry, net-
work of worts, will speak the climax in midsummer;
    how oaks will carry on and on, defying
denouement, the blank page after "The End."

Why is my father standing in the canoe
    like Jesus on his lake of lilies & listeners?
Father in his tomb of bones whole books
    ago? Summoned by green and words, Irish
father, preacher who wrote God on primroses
    and nettles, first chapter to last of his life.
Pitcher, preacher; words blend in the content

of this boat illustrated now by sun, birds
    shuttling over, shadows of worlds resurrected,
and me, learning to speak again the litany
    hanging here like mists of his old land tangled
in subterranean roots to this old land.
    No monks in monasteries need translate, or tribal
chiefs: *earth, air, fire, water* —

writing to rock any boat, and do.

Illuminated Page: Kellsian Fragment
in the Pine Barrens of New Jersey

The creek
speaks quietly beside
a silence lovely brimmed
with just belief, that creed
trembling on the tendril
splashing up from weeds
and greenly reaching.

I am moved to an assumption
of the daily bones and beads
of one scribe working
to set down the way it was,
am here to write
whatever sense may seep
into tendons untangling
from overshout and kill.
The swathe of scene before,
around, me, is the margin
everything illumines.

My time here's too little
to understand the squirrel's
astonishing wingless flight,
his centuries' spring and hover
there on a twig of pitch pine.
Or bluejays, bluebells, sounding
like saintly hours
on the stare of frogs —
names of all the world
we know, held, still.

I think how the monk's
habit itchy with lice
and probably lust
held him to a discipline

of doves and gaudy riot
running round luxurious,
and paradoxical, trappings
of God. Matthew, John.
The Christ Himself luminously
sad, the scintillating
cross . . . Look, a human
hand's more comfortable with
less blinding visions. I think
the singing knots and links
caught in Kells,
the skittery wild and somehow
tamed yet never tamed
woodfey, bogshy creatures
were divined as dance,
wine-inspired dreams in blood
too stately wedded, bedazzled
by spring's annunciations
and splendid blasphemies.

Now on my page a heron
drifts its shadow riffled
by wind, like the wing
of a god crossing, recrossing,
blurring distinctions, the weather
of something a man simply
scribing his life fired
into mine trying to find
an essential minimum.

The base metal must be
an assumption of faith.

II

Birches: Peterborough, New Hampshire

Frost, in a Vermont landscape, set them
sounding in our heads. Them? I prefer
the individual. Each shadow
reminds you of something by Mahler—note
after note dramatic, poignant, edged
with pain, the search for something beyond

the visible. A dusting of snow blown from
an evergreen changes all colors. Not to white.
Nothing is ever so pure or simplistic.
Look at bark mottled with music
from another opus, an opera Chekhov
might have considered writing, full

of humanity's everyday strivings for cherries
to sweeten the mundane meal. I mean,
a squirrel trills up the trunk chasing
nothing eye can follow, but the birch
barely perceptibly tolls tones
that tremble the whole forest of bones

in your body. You can't call it joy or sorrow;
this is ancient, pre-notation, but you hold
on to the fact that it is all
there is, welling up for you
again, again, from the center you know
is flame eternally flinting stars.

One Kind of Bestiary

"Born of the sun they traveled a short while
towards the sun, And left the vivid air signed with
their honor."

STEPHEN SPENDER

1. Day's End

Midnight. The station signing off. Sturm
und Drang drifting its drama starward, clanging
down channels of the ear which does not think
sleep. Nightcap. Another. Greying the moon,
an owl. Wolfbay hazing the hovering music.
In my glass the small glacier retreats.
I sip to nothing, snuff my light. Distant,
nearer, creatures sound the dark. Choir
of kin singly dying to that dark?
Bones burn out of blackness, shaping shadow.

2. Woolly Mammoth (Elephas primigenius)

The pits. Lined with boulders, scoured out
by glaciers, natural traps trembling immense
feet to falling. Wind combs through uncombed
hair of an astonished hulk remembering
looser air, ramming its roars on rock
ears of hunters hearing only *food*,
carving only *kill* on sharp stone points.
There is more than one last trumpet. Hacked to husk,
curved tusks a comma in time, beasts
notate frozen song, embedded elegies.

3. Auroch (Bos primigenius): European Wild Ox

1620 and a single pilgrim
twirls the Polish moon on six-foot high
horns, accepts the sun in eyes hoarding
history like a vault. Julius Caesar

34

adds to Empire forests of Gaul, beasts
not bulls or bison. It doesn't ease fleshache
to swirl round Charlemagne's stomach. No Crusaders,
oxen, grazing as that gang grasps towards God.
Philosophical question. If eyes no longer see
sun, does sun exist, sweet acorns age?

4. Quagga (Equus Quagga)

1883. An old survivor
dreaming, sinks finally into final bones,
seeing, perhaps, ancestors over a veldt
pool admiring fine striped heads, lithe
light brown bodies, legs white as clouds
they idly lap. Hottentots catch shrill barks:
quah*kah*, quah*kah*. Neighs nuzzle grass
too fancied by farmers. Kill, kill, *they* bark
out of their iron mouths, and the old female
in Amsterdam smudges a zoo's long dust.

5. Elephant Bird (Aepyornis Maximus)

Sinbad, I always believed your songs, trek
in huge talons to a fabled island.
Marco Polo spoke this true: ". . . like
an eagle . . . wings covered . . . thirty paces
. . . quills 12 paces long . . . will seize an elephant . . .
carry him high in the air . . ." A thousand pounds
weight, we read. Rock. Roc-like, you
clawed for only space, forest habitat
sawed to smaller, unwinged contours, concepts.
Skeletons, sail your tales on turning seas.

6. Day

Dawn. Demanding tapestry. Movement still
on the eye: auk, pigeons passing, silks
brilliant and tenuous. Blinking, I move to weave
myself into another day, worn

by that night watch. A bluejay blares green
treefrills trembling light. Trembling light.
If tomorrow's sun probes no promises spinning
in simple eyes, no sun exists, *I* say
for those who cannot say it. Which morning star
will see the jay's last impertinent shining?

Canzone for Constellations

Well, for stars, at least, those winks in sky
that say there's something there, as over water
bobbing lights speak out of blackness, sky
lights withheld by clouds. Unclouded, *sky*
writes itself on water, and by fire
centuries cold. I am rowing through sky
tales materializing from a sky
just inching dark. The boat is like an island
uprooted, shifting. Will it meld with land
elsewhere or drift through water-lilied sky
forever, moving over shapes of light
my paddle touches, cannot move? Alight

with myths reflected, tickled by a light
breeze, the pond moves in my bones, I sky
and all its stories, syllables of light
speaking time, *keeping* time. The leit-
motif is Greek, nuggets of land all water-
locked where I am beached. Clearest light
falls here in rarest colors. After daylight,
headier light. I read the points of fire
burning eyes. There on paws of fire,
by fired wings, Pegasus leaps light
as air the world. I see his hoof touch land,
see Hippocrene on Helicon, high land

of Muses, spring up, see him whir to land
to sip at Corinth's essence, see shining light
of golden bridle, and him mastered. Skyland,
you give me hunters for my blander land.
Look how, lion-skinned, he strides the sky.
Orion! Apollo swept him from a land
of love and loss to that eternal land
he claims by club. He laps in gentle water
as I watch, three bright stars in water
compass to his country. A hero's land

is Hercules' just there near Vega's fire.
I see him labor, blood and bones on fire,

and after conquering all, no end of fire
flaming him to exploits scorching land
and sea until, torched himself by fire,
he kneels on heaven's altar, holding fire
still. I, a woman, search light
for women by following fields of dark. Fire
is a "W", is a Queen on fire,
Cassiopeia, ruling a corner of sky
lucidly. She sired in that sky
most brilliant Nova on a throne of fire
fish hold in their eyes. They turn in water
I turn in. Below, above, water

is a world. Dippers hold black water
here, there, pails of only fire.
Myriad points waver on this water,
movements of those swimming in *that* water—
water bearer treading his rare land,
creatures beautiful in any water:
fish, a shining crab. Over water
now a pour of music, lyric light
soundless as it sings. By such light
sailors go or find the homing water
surer than by fallible man's. Sky
on fire, how you fire inner sky.

The paddle rings against a rock sky-
flinted, too, clangs me to known water:
pond, not Grecian sea and sands of fire.
I row towards shore, dreamer from dappled island
odysseys strummed on lines of light.

Message to Other Civilizations: Bach

> *When asked what news he would send to other*
> *civilizations, Lewis Thomas, author of* The Medusa
> and The Snail, *said, "I would send the complete*
> *works of J.S. Bach. But that would be boasting."*
> *Bach works* were *sent on a disc into space under*
> *the aegis of Carl Sagan.*

In the cozy tangle of twenty children
you never could have imagined
sailing on a disc through your God's heavens,
golden, in a slipcase of aluminum, shimmering
like angels' wings.

Through rings of moon and Saturn, past Jupiter
to unnamed stars, you spin
simplistically as snow soft on Saint
Thomas' Church in Leipzig of a Sunday.
You tossed off a cantata for the service.

      Then: *out of fashion*
          we've gone beyond baroque

Old tale. You forgotten,
much of your music lost
by little minds.

New star, the nineteenth century
beamed, and you in your old luminous mantle
whirled from darkness

as you whirl now out into deep space—
you never could have imagined? You
lived in that infinity always, heard
harmonies there fingering over your bones
like fugues of light.

With Sagan's blessing you will swirl for sixty
thousand years and more, unmarked
by meteorites, though you will mark all bodies
there as you have ours. They've sent you, merely,
Godlike, home.

Version: Old Tale, After the Grimms

Already the pond understands a silken skin
yet too tenuous for passage. The moon
offers itself wholly. Silos,
fields gaunt, contain
creakings, whimperings
of skeletal mice. You can imagine two
children, hand in hand, believing
in the compass of crumbs,
can hear, almost, a hag
huzzahing in her long hair, twisting
taffy for sills, slates.

And the woman, elsewhere, gathering
her narrow harvest, loosing
her lank prayers, is arrested
by a slither of owl,
bones
feathered for flight,
the moon turning white
stones the prints
of a deer she does not see
even now spinning,
flint-hooved,
home.

Illuminations: Fish

They hang under ice
as if asleep, in dreams

hearing perhaps
the sink of limb shadows,

from a miry womb, fantasies
of peeper eggs imagining what

they will become, fronds
moaning at moon-knock, a stone

shifting in something like wind
more like remembrance of wave.

Their heads may sing with sound
in that tingled globe.

It is always the way,
silence an illusion

like frost in the bone
already phrasing: *flowers*

III

The Exceptional Child

pinballs round the room tilting
everything over or smashed. He flails
fists into the cat. What figure
does she assume to him? A devil,
ten spears bared to sliver his brain
that bends in unfathomable byways?

Stilled with a needle, he pants.
A skein of saliva puddles the floor
the moon floats in, fractured. I think
of the night he was made, the tangled stars
in the maple, the slithering coil of genes,
marred, and sweet as perfection. His eyes
cringe as I kiss them. Why does he break
my bones with tears that thud like stones?

Simplicity's Dimensions

A friend phones: *my daughter's diagnosed*
retarded. What can I answer, dusk diminishing
wet-bright colors as time the Sistine ceiling?

Two weeks ago I read of Verdi's retarded
sister. I see her beside her father, the poor
innkeeper, arranging bouquets for deal tables:
nasturtium's common grace, a sprig of wild
garlic for spice. Not far away fields
of wheat offer wind a mellow home
on its way to Florence, city of flowers
and frescoes. Once I stood on Ponte Vecchio
over the Arno holding shadows, art
in shades of grey, not ephemeral, etched
forever in the ancient river, for who can say
because shades fade they are not saved in some
dimension of the mystery this world is?

Here is a girl standing beside a sun-brushed
doorway, hands pungent with garlic's gusto.
Cypress tones from the shadowy collective
spill over her Fra Angelico, Dante, Giotto.
Wind twists in her long black hair scent
of lilies massed in the Sistine where now a man
is recovering from darkness *light* as two fingers touch
in the high silence a man in another city
seizes, in solitude, creation's necessary element.
His *Requiem* was for Manzoni, scholars say.
I say it was, too, for a sister, glorious
as bells in an old campanile offering overtones
to God brisk in a buttercup she bends to pick.

I will say to my friend: think of shadows' shifting
dimensions, how opera means works, on a ceiling or a city
of flowers arranged carefully for light's revelations.

Picture of Victims of Famine

You think how far they have come
to this: salons
offering diets of dust, insistence
on calesthenics, twist
and grip of the gut, the reaching
arms, fingers nimbled
for foraging.

In the foreground
a child is all eyes, rich
blackberries
pressed juiceless, belly
bloated like a moon, full
of dead masses.

How small dots
in newsprint buzz,
flies at a festering. They move
only in the mind. You know
no sound ebbs
from any thing, and this
is only a map. Even now

archeologists spade
through piles of paper, unearthing
grants: monies green, nourishing.

Then the real dig, the release
to light, the careful
catalogue, sifted fine:
lamentations, testaments
of bone, relics — whose
death, this decadence?

Looking at a Pompeiian Lady in an Exhibit

Everywhere the spill
of summer, air cracked
by only birdbells, sails
moving like old dances.

At her lips you imagine
china, thin as a peeling of star,
thoughts unfocused
as flittering butterflies:

is her son (too young)
kissing in some carriage,
will her husband stir
slack breasts tonight,
should she offer
figs, what wine
will most please?

The flow is gentle
in the mind, lazy
pour of dustmotes.

How lips poised to sip
hold the set of summer
still
and you wait for words,
a froth of grace to guests:

>   *Shall we walk round the garden?*
>   *Isn't the season gay this year?*

all your shouted urgencies
bubbles breaking soundless
on a glassy sea, she
smiling on, you
writhing, banging *run*.

Thoughts on Reading of the Altar of Silkworms Where Women Used to Pray, Forbidden City, Peking

Something like waterslip over rocks in a river
burred by sun, the slurred movement of bodies
towards mulberry trees in a grove. On women's lips
prayers like threads for the soft spinning.

What is the secret weave they work towards heaven
glimpsed through the mottled glow?

Wings. Wrestling free, they brush
with unfettered feet shoals of stars, sands
of moon. See in wind they go, iridescent
moths stitched on bluest sky, even as,
below the dream, stuttering feet
seek peace in the flow of yin, yang,
in cocoons they pray will split, seasoned,
loose rustling filaments. Their eyes lift up
to the immeasurable space
between the light-touched leaves.

Poem for Charlotte Mew
Who Burned Many of Her Poems
Before Her Death

Cold fires burn deepest,
light a steam of frost that blots us out.

Your room mists into my mind. Ornate-framed
faces crowd space like atoms; patterned
cloths drop from every table genteel
as need. On a footstool by the grate
you scratch poems. From flint,
ice, they feed on you, are fed,
ravenous Ibex come from heights
only imagined. Fog films my sight.
I do not see you burn imperfect beasts
but even when I have shut your door, all doors,
sealed every window, stopped my ears, I hear
their high slim cries, a shattering out of the bone,

and in their black disintegration see
you at the center, dead
by your own hand, dust
over the moors a scatter of fired frost.

Schooldays at the University of Alabama

"Tuscaloosa: A Tense Drama Unfolds"

NEW YORK TIMES MAGAZINE,
Feb. 26, 1956

I want a moment of silence
for Autherine Lucy,
her jangling bones as she walked
the pot-holed road to her destiny,
scared fauns in her eyes
hidden by bravery's brush
for her feet that squirmed
for a different road, one that had
nothing to do with demi-gods riding
floats of power and prejudice,
one concerned only with learning
how the brain can hold,
juxtaposed,
equations and estuaries.

Now.
One moment of silence.
Please.

For remembrance of how it was
hard.

A Viewer, Wednesday, February 8, 1587, Scotland

Through slits in stone iced meadows took the eye,
and early snowdrops drifting over small
shadows. Good cheer sang in my bones. A sprawl
of us, the insignificant, among them I,
were given boon: the chance to watch her die.

I'd brought a skin of wine. The thing might pall;
you never knew. I settled in. The hall
filled up with dignitaries, some low, most high.
A huge fire took chill's edge. A sudden sigh.
One great breath sucked. It was our own. Tall,
gowned in satin, black, her hair a fall
of auburn a fine white veil softened, dry-
eyed, stiffly proud, she floated in. No eye
strayed from that figure. She held the hall in thrall,
grande dame, a Queen, and in command, all
dignity as she bent down to die.

She stripped off black. Lord! Laced in red
she blazed from toes to bodice. The block, the blade
never stirred her smile. Her women cried,
not she. "Ne crie point pour moi," she said.
I needed no translation.

                    Unafraid
the eyes white-clothed, she blocked her neck, the guide
her own sure hands, and prayed. The slice fell wide,
just grazed her head. The lips still softly prayed.
The next blow severed, except for slender bits
of sinew. These sawed, the thing was raised. Stark-eyed,
I stared. The head fell free, the red wig stayed.

That homeless head writhed words full fifteen minutes.

Dover, the Present Time, Looking Towards Dunkirk

May sun shimmers the ship. I watch it go
spry as a gull it flies under on its wing
of only air, hovering in a glow
of moving light like some god-conjured thing.
Amazing craft, sitting a span of sea
wraithes walk in burning oil miraculously.
Miraculously it feathers towards Calais
in snap-of-fingers time, flaring spray
like a jeweled fan flicked by a racy belle.
What is this place, this sun, this innocent bay?
White cliffs, are these your bones, haven from hell?

The pilgrim is half fool, time his foe
glossing glorious through haze, hallowing
a putrid depth of deeds become our woe
that fog-dark night, Dunkirk a baleful flaming
crescent on the horizon. I'd left my tea,
steaming, to notify the Admiralty
I had a launch I'd lend to make the foray—
small but hearty. The British underplay
most serious things. A lark, a bagatelle
to church-in-the-dunes, a known beach, short sway
from the haven of white cliffs' sweeping bones. Hell,

I discovered, thumbs its nose at death, that blow
too lusted after, dances, prances, leering
at crippled fired docks and decks. Slow,
almost stalled in time, we took on staring
burnt-black men, layering them gently
as bombcrack overhead allowed, many
beyond capacity's wisdom. What would *you* say
to agony's eyes silently screaming? Our way
from the beach was a crimson clutter of boats, a knell
of sound and light like a devil's Judgment Day.
O white cliffs, ring your bones, haven from hell.

Homebound in dark beyond dark, I cringed at the flow
of lifeboats deadmen manned, silently slipping
to God knew where, at the terrible clutching show
of hands we could never grasp. In bombs' numbing
thud the whine of mad dogs, horses free
on the beach trampling corpses, make memory
a tomb of terrible ghosts. Through that decay
we steamed, too low in the water, engines astray,
oil, blood, and flesh-fouled, towards the tell
toppling chalky to a sweet-shoaled cay:
white cliffs, the ring of their bones haven from hell.

If I could have imagined a flying boat to tow
crazed fragmented men to the clasp and cling
of mothering cliffs, I would have shaped your low
clean hull saving breath, outdistancing
at least some spectres. We limped to Dover's lea.
Men lidless, lame, some limbless, moved sluggishly
ashore to teacarts' comfort, a quiet display
of decency to dull the demons of fray.
Forty some years ago! A minute. I dwell
more on it now; the past becomes today.
White cliffs you ring old bones, no haven from hell.

Envoy:

Another mist sifts in. From that fine grey
they move again, majestic in this May,
divine in simple duty. From bowels, a bell
tolls long tones for that dear waste. I pray.
Cliffs white with bones ring this: all war is hell.

Ballade by an Old Jewish Woman

We make choices. I can either cry
or make a kind of song. I choose to play
notes in my head that, anyway, (try
as I do for silence), sing night and day.
This, then, is a staff, or so we may say,
though somehow it seems wrong. How can I claim
five parallel lines can capture the jagged way
we died while living faceless, without names?

Connotations crowd. Furtive, I pry
a crust of bread from a dead hand grey
in light greying to black blacker than eye
saw before or since, and eat it, gay
(terribly, fiercely) at how I've held at bay,
a filthy second, hunger's beasts. Word game.
Stave, not *staff of life*. A madman's prey,
we died while living faceless, without names.

Still, I mean to sing. The younger I
remembers a wide windowsill, sway
of light on one Berlin bird spring-high
on sweetest air before his perfect lay
turned dirge heard in another place . . . I stray.
To make a music of it was my aim,
nothing maudlin, for then I would betray
who died while living faceless, without names.

Smudges on the page. Aging, how can I convey
that dissonance, that world aflame, I who came
back by miracle? With this mission: *Remember,* I pray,
who died while living faceless, without names.

Tour of Seegrotte Caves Near Vienna

We unravel from the bus,
forty eager foreigners.
Vendors hawk. Billboard maps
paint depths, dimensions
of dark to come. The mouth,
indifferent hole in earth's face,
receives us.

Single file cuts conversation.
Some put hands on shoulders
of the one in front
until we stutter
into a cavern wide
as a dozen rooms.
Lights of candles quiver,
shadows slither on dripping walls.

     "Here Germans manufactured
     planes using labor
     from concentration camps."

Chill clots blood.
Damp sifts into roots
of teeth. The seeping odor
is decay.

     How many months?
     How many years?

We twist
to an underground river.
Smiling boatman.
You will enjoy. Most do
joke, jostle as we slip
on icy water in half-light

past niches, coffins
of burnt-out candles.

Caves give back sound
eerily. In my head
cries, moans, wails, frozen
behind faces sculptured
for survival.

We surface to spring light
soft as prayers
they dared not voice.

For Venice, Sinking

to a former companion

"No man is an island." True, but parts of peninsulas
and capes of known islands bump in the blood
like all canzone ever uttered, hovering
invisibly in air over mud
clusters tenuously tethered by root
or less to the Adriatic's mottled azure.

Metric is not my medium. What does a kilo
do to a mile's dimensions? As for milli-
anything, who can compute that spacious modicum?
Festooned with lights, boats wander old space
in my mind. Feast of the Redentore. Singing.
Does light raise or lessen a canal's level?

Stone bridges centuries. Gabble of trade
Babels the Rialto, retreats to Sighs
before a Palace doges played, and you
with me argued Tintoretto's, Titian's
and Veronese's values layered defter
than our love to last. "Only art,"

someone shrugged last night over wine
and words about the stealthy slip to water's
wily elements. "Think of Biafra, think
of boat people blurring to dawn, in a trice
spilled beyond communion's comfort, think
of Pompeii, think of our own Blue & Grey . . ."

So I thought, and thought how I could love
them back and couldn't, thought how I could float
a candle, avenues, whole counties of candles
for their souls down streams of tears and time
which too is islands linked by art's long chain.
How else probe a Shylock, suffer Dante's

loss and gain? My old grandfather clock
speaks like St. Mark's campanile, sings
you from other time, in your passionate gestures
containing a moment the ticking. I tear a print
from a fading book: moon-flooded stones. Tacked up
it's a milli-something below eye level, and bothers.

You're not here to notice, but purist, romantic, despite
deficiencies in measuring foreign units,
I tinker to true, see immeasurable pigeons
stuffed on an old square's debris, how they crowd
column and cornice against night's chill calculations.
Individual vision only? It *matters*, in time.

Photo by Kathleen Frank

Geraldine C. Little, born in Ireland, now lives in Mt. Holly, N.J. She is Vice President of The Poetry Society of America and a past president of The Haiku Society of America. She has published a book-length narrative poem on the incarceration of Japanese-Americans during World War II, *Hakugai* (persecution). Her awards include five from The Poetry Society of America, an AWP Anniversary Award, a PEN Syndicated Short Fiction Award, as well as two grants in poetry and one in prose from The New Jersey State Council on the Arts. She is a Fellow of The MacDowell Colony. A teacher and musician, she sings with The Choral Arts Society of Philadelphia, performing with The Philadelphia Orchestra.